Praise for

How the West Brought War to Ukraine

"A brilliant, remarkably concise explanation of the danger that U.S. and NATO military involvement in Ukraine has created. Needs to be read and pondered by every citizen capable of thinking rationally and responsibly about American and European security."
— **Jack F. Matlock, Jr.**, U.S. Ambassador to the Soviet Union, 1987-1991, author of *Superpower Illusions*

"This is a splendid little book, tautly written, logically organized, easy to read, and persuasive but appropriately caveated. It is an invaluable primer on the trends and events that produced the escalating warfare in Ukraine. Without understanding the history documented in this book, there will be no de-escalation of the U.S.-Russian confrontation on Europe's eastern borders."
— **Chas Freeman**, previously Assistant Secretary of Defense for International Security Affairs, author of *Arts of Power: Statecraft and Diplomacy*

"For those concerned about U.S. national security and the peace of Europe, this book is essential reading."
— **Douglas Macgregor**, Colonel (Retired), U.S. Army, author of *Margin of Victor*, was decorated for valor in the Battle of 73 Easting in Iraq and served as Director of NATO's Joint Operations Center at SHAPE (Supreme Headquarters Allied Powers Europe)

"For anyone interested in understanding the true causes of the disaster in Ukraine, *How the West Brought War to Ukraine* is required reading. Abelow makes a clear and compelling case that the United States and its NATO allies—not Vladimir Putin—are the principal culprits."

—**John J. Mearsheimer**, author of *The Tragedy of Great Power Politics*, is the R. Wendell Harrison Distinguished Service Professor of Political Science at the University of Chicago

"A concise yet comprehensive and accessible overview. Invaluable for understanding how war once again came to Europe. Benjamin Abelow demonstrates that the crisis in Ukraine was predictable, predicted—and avoidable."

—**Richard Sakwa**, author of *Frontline Ukraine* and *The Putin Paradox*, is Professor of Russian and European Politics, University of Kent

"Ben Abelow takes us beyond the false narratives and into the truth of the Ukraine crisis."

—**Krishen Mehta**, Senior Global Justice Fellow, Yale University, and Director, American Committee for US-Russia Accord

"In the Ukraine proxy war between the United States/NATO and Russia, we face a threat of nuclear escalation that could end human civilization. Abelow's book is essential reading for all who wish to understand this threat and why, 30 years after the collapse of the Soviet Union, it has re-emerged."

—**Gilbert Doctorow**, author of *Memoirs of a Russianist*, is an historian and independent Russia specialist based in Brussels Headquarters Allied Powers Europe)

HOW THE WEST BROUGHT WAR TO UKRAINE

HOW THE WEST BROUGHT WAR TO UKRAINE

UNDERSTANDING HOW U.S. AND NATO
POLICIES LED TO CRISIS, WAR, AND
THE RISK OF NUCLEAR CATASTROPHE

BENJAMIN ABELOW

S
P
Siland Press
Great Barrington, Massachusetts, USA

Siland Press
Great Barrington, Massachusetts
Info@SilandPress.com

Disclaimer: Careful efforts have been made to ensure the accuracy of the information contained in this book. However, because human error can occur, and because underlying source documents or secondary sources sometimes contain mistakes, no guarantee can be offered about the accuracy of everything contained herein.

Cover design by Boja@99designs.

ISBN: 978-0-9910767-0-3

Library of Congress Control Number: 2022911492

Publisher's Cataloging-in-Publication Data

Names: Abelow, Benjamin, author

Title: How the West brought war to Ukraine : understanding how U.S. and NATO policies led to crisis, war, and the risk of nuclear catastrophe / Benjamin Abelow

Description: [Great Barrington, Massachusetts] : Siland Press, [2022] | Includes bibliographical references and index.

Identifiers: ISBN: 978-0-9910767-0-3 (paperback) | 978-0-9910767-1-0 (ebook) | LCCN: 2022911492

Subjects: LCSH: Ukraine Conflict, 2014- | United States—Foreign relations—Russia (Federation) | North Atlantic Treaty Organization. | North Atlantic Treaty Organization—Ukraine. | Europe—Foreign relations—Russia (Federation)—21st century. | Western countries—Foreign relations—Russia (Federation)—21st century. | National security—Europe. | National security—United States. | Russia (Federation)—Foreign relations—21st century. | Security, International—Europe—History—21st century. | Cuban Missile Crisis, 1962. | South Ossetia War, 2008. | Nuclear arms control. | Nuclear crisis control. | Nuclear warfare. | Geopolitics. | Baltic States—Strategic aspects. | World politics. | International relations. | Political science. | BISAC: HISTORY / Wars & Conflicts / General. | POLITICAL SCIENCE / International Relations / General. | POLITICAL SCIENCE / Security (National & International) | POLITICAL SCIENCE / World / Russian & Former Soviet Union.

Classification: LCC: DK508.852 .A24 2022 | DDC: 947.7086--dc23

Acknowledgements

For answering technical questions, commenting on previous drafts, or providing other kinds of help, I wish to thank Major Brennan Deveraux, Jay R. Feierman, Richard Sakwa, Gilbert Doctorow, George Goss, Viktoryia Baum, Pam Auerbach, Mark McCarty, John Hayden, Alex Tabarrok, Adam Abelow, Kimberly Peticolas, and Jonathan Rubin. The inclusion of a name here does not imply endorsement of the ideas expressed in this book. All views, as well as any errors of fact, interpretation, or judgment, are the sole responsibility of the author.

Contents

Overview

For almost 200 years, starting with the framing of the Monroe Doctrine in 1823, the United States has asserted security claims over virtually the whole Western hemisphere. Any foreign power that places military forces near U.S. territory knows it is crossing a red line. U.S. policy thus embodies a conviction that *where* a potential opponent places its forces is crucially important. In fact, this conviction is the cornerstone of American foreign and military policy, and its violation is considered reason for war.

Yet when it comes to Russia, the United States and its NATO allies have acted for decades in disregard of this same principle. They have progressively advanced the placement of their military forces toward Russia, even to its borders. They have done this with inadequate attention to, and sometimes blithe disregard for, how Russian leaders might perceive this advance. Had Russia taken equivalent actions with respect to U.S. territory — say, placing its military forces in Canada or Mexico — Washington would have gone to war and justified that war as a defensive response to the military encroachment of a foreign power.

When viewed through this lens, Russia's invasion of Ukraine is seen not as the unbridled expansionism of a malevolent Russian leader but as a violent and destructive reaction to misguided Western policies: an attempt to reestablish a zone around Russia's western border that is free of offensive threats from the United States and its allies. Having misunderstood why Russia invaded Ukraine, the West is now basing existential decisions on false premises. In doing so, it is deepening the crisis and may be sleepwalking toward nuclear war.

This argument, which I now present in detail, is based on the analyses of a number of scholars, government officials, and military observers, all of whom I introduce and quote from in the course of the presentation. These include John Mearsheimer, Stephen F. Cohen, Richard Sakwa, Gilbert Doctorow, George F. Kennan, Chas Freeman, Douglas Macgregor, and Brennan Deveraux.

Introduction:
How the Narrative Drives the War

In the months since Russia invaded Ukraine, the explanation offered for America's involvement has changed. What had been pitched as a limited, humanitarian effort to help Ukraine defend itself has morphed to include an additional aim: to degrade Russia's capacity to fight another war in the future.

In fact, this strategic objective may have been in place from the start. In March, more than a month before the new U.S. policy was announced, Chas Freeman, previously Assistant Secretary of Defense for International Security Affairs, observed,

> Everything we are doing, rather than accelerating an end to the fighting and some compromise, seems to be aimed at prolonging the fighting, assisting the Ukrainian resistance — which is a noble cause, I suppose, but ... will result in a lot of dead Ukrainians as well as dead Russians.[1]

Freeman's observation points to an uncomfortable truth: America's two war aims are not really compatible with each other. Whereas a humanitarian effort would seek to limit the destruction and end the war quickly, the strategic goal of weakening Russia requires a prolonged war with maximum destruction, one that bleeds Russia dry of men and machine on battlefield Ukraine. Freeman captures the contradiction in a darkly ironic quip: "We will fight to the last Ukrainian for Ukrainian independence."

America's new military objective places the United States into a posture of direct confrontation with Russia. Now the goal is to cripple a part of the Russian state, its military. Since the start of the war, the Biden administration and Congress have allocated over 50 billion dollars in aid for Ukraine, the majority of it military. U.S. officials have revealed that American intelligence enabled the killing of a dozen Russian generals in Ukraine, as well as the sinking of the *Moskva*, the flagship of Russia's Black Sea fleet, killing 40 sailors and wounding 100. America's European allies fell into line, greatly increasing the number and lethality of the weapons they are shipping. British leaders have sought to expand the battlefield, openly encouraging the Ukrainian military to use Western weapons to attack supply lines inside Russia.

On February 27, three days after the Russian invasion began, Russian president Vladimir Putin announced that, in response to "aggressive statements" from Western leaders, he had raised the alert status of Russia's nuclear forces. In May, a close media associate of Mr. Putin warned the British prime minister that his statements and actions risk subjecting England to a radioactive tsunami from one of Russia's land-attack nuclear torpedoes. This and other Russian warnings about nuclear war have been dismissed by most of the Western media as mere propaganda. Yet within 24 hours of Mr. Putin's February 27 announcement, the U.S. military raised its alert status to Defcon 3 for the first time since the 2001 attack on the World Trade Towers.[2] The result is that both countries are closer to a hair-trigger launch policy, increasing the chance that an accident, political miscalculation, or computer error could lead to a nuclear exchange.

Further, one must consider what would happen if Russia started to lose, and its overall military capacity was degraded to the point where Moscow perceived itself as vulnerable to invasion. In that situation, Russian planners would surely contemplate using low-yield battlefield nuclear weapons to destroy enemy forces. Thus, the U.S. Director of National Intelligence, in testimony before the Senate Armed Services Committee in May, stated that Mr. Putin might use nuclear weapons if there was "an existential threat to his regime and to Russia, from his perspective." This could occur if "he perceives he is losing the war."[3] If Russia did use nuclear weapons, the pressure for a Western nuclear response, followed by further escalation, might be irresistible. Yet that situation — Russian loss and depletion — *is exactly what the new U.S. policy is seeking to achieve.*

Finally, we must ask what would happen if the war dragged on to the point where opposition to Mr. Putin within Russian elites led to his removal from power. Here we are talking about the vaunted goal of "regime change," which in the United States is sought by an informal alliance of Republican neoconservatives and Democratic liberal interventionists. The assumption seems to be that Mr. Putin would be replaced by a docile, effete puppet subservient to American interests. Gilbert Doctorow—an independent, Brussels-based political analyst whose Ph.D. and post-doctoral training are in Russian history—comments:

> Be careful what you wish for. Russia has more nuclear weapons than the United States. Russia has more modern weapons than the United States. Russia can level to the

ground the United States in 30 minutes. Is this a country in which you want to create turmoil? Moreover, if [Mr. Putin] were to be overturned, who would take his place? Some little namby-pamby? Some new drunkard like [first Russian president Boris] Yeltsin? Or somebody who is a Rambo and just ready to push the button? ... I think it is extremely imprudent for a country like the United States to invoke regime change in a country like Russia. It's almost suicidal.[4]

Whether or not eviscerating Russia's military has been the American plan from the outset, the policy is not surprising because it follows logically, even predictably, from an overarching Western narrative about Russia that has already been widely accepted. According to this narrative, Mr. Putin is an insatiable expansionist who lacks any plausible national security motivations for his decisions. This narrative portrays Mr. Putin as a new Hitler, and the Russian move into Ukraine as akin to the Nazi aggression of World War II. Likewise, the narrative portrays any Western desire to compromise and negotiate a quick end to the conflict as wishful thinking and appeasement. America's new military objective thus emerges directly from Western perceptions about Moscow's motivations and the causes of the war.

And so a crucial question comes into focus: Is the Western narrative about the Ukraine war correct? If it is, then Western policies might arguably make sense, even if they entail some risk of nuclear conflict. But if the narrative is wrong, then the West is basing existential decisions on false premises. If the narrative is wrong, a quickly negotiated compromise, one that would spare the lives of combatants and civilians alike, and simultaneously greatly reduce the risk of nuclear war, would not represent appeasement. Rather, it would be a practical necessity, even a moral obligation. Finally, if the Western narrative about Russia's motivations is wrong, then the actions the West is taking now are likely to deepen the crisis and may lead to nuclear war.

In this book, I argue that the Western narrative is incorrect. In crucial respects, it is the opposite of truth. The underlying cause of the war lies not in an unbridled expansionism of Mr. Putin, or in paranoid delusions of military planners in the Kremlin, but in a 30-year history of Western provocations, directed at Russia, that began during the dissolution of the Soviet Union and continued to the start of the war. These provocations placed Russia in an untenable situation, for which war seemed, to Mr. Putin and his military staff, the only workable solution. In arguing this case, I pay special attention to the United States — and subject it to particularly sharp criticism— because it has played the decisive role in shaping Western policy.

In criticizing the West, it is not my aim to justify Moscow's invasion or exonerate Russia's leaders. I have no brief for Mr. Putin. Notwithstanding all I will say, I believe he had alternatives to war. But I do want to *understand* him—in the sense of seeking to rationally assess the causal sequence that led him to launch the war.

What do I have in mind when I speak of Western provocations? It is often suggested that the expansion of NATO into the countries of Eastern Europe has contributed to tensions. This assertion is correct but incomplete. To begin with, the implications of NATO expansion too often remain abstractions, with the actual threat to Russia not appreciated. At the same time, the United States and its allies, both individually and in coordination with one another, have taken provocative military actions that are not directly tied to NATO. Focusing on NATO is important, but attending only to NATO obscures the full scope and seriousness of the predicament that the West has created for Russia.

As a preview for what is to come, I list here key Western provocations, which I will explain and comment on over the course of this book. During the past three decades, the United States, sometimes alone, sometimes with its European allies, has done the following:

- Expanded NATO over a thousand miles eastward, pressing it toward Russia's borders, in disregard of assurances previously given to Moscow

- Withdrawn unilaterally from the Antiballistic Missile Treaty and placed antiballistic launch systems in newly joined NATO countries. These launchers can also accommodate and fire offensive nuclear weapons at Russia, such as nuclear-tipped Tomahawk cruise missiles

- Helped lay the groundwork for, and may have directly instigated, an armed, far-right coup in Ukraine. This coup replaced a democratically elected pro-Russian government with an unelected pro-Western one

- Conducted countless NATO military exercises near Russia's border. These have included, for example, live-fire rocket exercises whose goal was to simulate attacks on air-defense systems inside Russia

- Asserted, without pressing strategic need, and in disregard of the threat such a move would pose for Russia, that Ukraine would become a NATO member. NATO then refused to renounce this policy even when doing so might have averted war

- Withdrawn unilaterally from the Intermediate-Range Nuclear Forces Treaty, increasing Russian vulnerability to a U.S. first strike

- Armed and trained the Ukrainian military through bilateral agreements and held regular joint military training exercises inside Ukraine. The goal has been to produce NATO-level military interoperability even before formally admitting Ukraine into NATO

- Led the Ukrainian leadership to adopt an uncompromising stance toward Russia, further exacerbating the threat to Russia and putting Ukraine in the path of Russian military blowback

Because of the depth of the crisis; because it evolved over a period of decades; and because thermonuclear war—a war fought with hydrogen bombs—entails an existential threat to all the countries involved, as well as to humanity at large, I will make my case as clearly and systematically as I can. I structure the book in eight short chapters, which build the argument in stepwise fashion.

Chapter 1 chronologically surveys Western provocations of Russia during the period 1990–2014. Chapter 2 extends this survey to the beginning of Russia's February 2022 invasion. Chapter 3 asks how the United States would react if "the shoe were on the other foot"—that is, if Russia acted toward the United States as the West has acted toward Russia. Chapter 4 describes the implications for Russian security of the American withdrawal from the 1987 intermediate-range nuclear missile treaty.

Chapter 5 explains how U.S. foreign policy experts publicly warned that NATO expansion would lead to disaster. Chapter 6 describes how those responsible for NATO's failed expansion policy are now doubling down on their mistakes. Chapter 7 explains how overly pessimistic perceptions about the intentions of potential opponents tend to become self-fulfilling prophecies. Chapter 8 presents a counterfactual history, considering what might have been had the West acted differently. Chapter 8 also addresses the question of who bears primary responsibility for the ongoing disaster in Ukraine.

1.

Western Provocations: 1990–2014

The story begins in 1990, when, as the Soviet Union was coming to an end, Western leaders sought to reunify East and West Germany under NATO's auspices. This required that Moscow agree to remove its roughly 400,000 troops from East Germany. To mollify Moscow, Western leaders communicated the view that NATO would not expand eastward toward Russia's border.

According to an analysis by the National Security Archive of George Washington University, where relevant declassified documents are posted, "a cascade of assurances about Soviet security [were] given by Western leaders to Gorbachev and other Soviet officials throughout the process of German unification in 1990 and on into 1991." These assurances pertained not only to the question of NATO's expansion into East Germany, as is sometimes asserted, but also to the expansion of NATO into the countries of Eastern Europe. Nonetheless, within a few years, NATO began to expand toward Russia's border. Although the assurances had not been instantiated in formal treaties, "subsequent Soviet and Russian complaints about being misled about NATO expansion" were not simply Russian propaganda but, rather, were "founded in written contemporaneous [memoranda] at the highest levels" of Western governments.[5]

A similar conclusion was reached by Joshua R. Shifrinson in the journal *International Security*. Shifrinson describes evidence that "the United States misled the Soviet Union" and violated the spirit of the negotiations.[6] In an interview at the Harvard Kennedy School's Belfer Center, Shifrinson described his archival research:

> I was able to see, simultaneously, what was being told to the Soviets to their faces and what the U.S. was telling itself in the back room. Many of the Russians...have repeatedly claimed that an informal non-expansion pledge was offered by the U.S. in 1990. And for the last 25 years, Western policy makers, at least in the U.S., have roundly said, "No, we didn't, and nothing was written down and it wasn't signed so it doesn't matter if [we] did." And what I found [in the archives] was that the Russian narrative is basically exactly what happened.[7]

In describing this episode, I am not suggesting that Western assurances were legally binding, or that the violation of these assurances fully explains Russia's invasion of Ukraine. In fact, the question of American, European, and Soviet discussions during 1990 and 1991 about NATO expansion is a subject of ongoing debate.[8] I simply want to note that the West acted in a way calculated to deceive Moscow, and that this episode laid the foundation for an evolving Russian sense that NATO, and the United States in particular, could not be trusted.

Although the trajectory of NATO expansion became clear in the mid-90s, the first decisive step occurred in 1999, when NATO formally admitted three new countries from Eastern Europe. In a recent interview, Army Colonel (retired) Douglas Macgregor, Ph.D., a storied Iraq commander who helped develop U.S. war plans for Europe, commented on the admission of one of these countries:

> [W]hen we decided in 1999 to bring in Poland…[t]he Russians were very worried — not so much because NATO was hostile at the time but because they knew that Poland was. Poland has a long history of hostility toward Russia…. Poland is, if anything, at this point in time, a potential catalyst for war with Russia.[9]

In 2001, two years after the admission of this first group of new NATO members, President George W. Bush unilaterally withdrew from the Antiballistic Missile (ABM) Treaty. Then, in 2004, NATO admitted additional East European countries, including Romania and Estonia, the latter of which borders on Russia. By this point, NATO had expanded close to a thousand miles toward Russia.

In 2008, at a NATO summit in Bucharest, Romania, NATO announced, in the so-called Bucharest Memorandum, that it intended to admit Ukraine and Georgia as members. Both countries border on Russia. Although European members of NATO had serious reservations, the administration of President George W. Bush used the position of the United States as senior member of the alliance to push the issue, and the following unequivocal statement was included in the memorandum: "We agreed today that these countries [Ukraine and Georgia] will become members of NATO." However, no formal action to actually admit those countries was taken.

From the start, Russia has viewed the possible entry of Ukraine and Georgia as existential threats. Ukraine shares a 1,200-mile land border with Russia, parts of which are just 400 miles from Moscow. In a 2008 cable sent to Washington, then-U.S. ambassador to Russia, William J. Burns, who currently is director of the CIA, described his meeting with the Russian foreign minister. Burns noted that Russia considered the entry of Ukraine and Georgia into NATO a line that could not be crossed. This fact was reflected in the heading Burns gave to his cable: "Nyet Means Nyet [No Means No]: Russia's NATO Enlargement Redlines." Burns wrote, "Not only does Russia perceive encirclement, and efforts to undermine Russia's influence in the region, but it also fears unpredictable and uncontrolled consequences which would seriously affect Russian security interests."[10]

In August 2008, four months after NATO's announcement about Ukraine and Georgia, Russia's military crossed into Georgia and entered into a brief war with Georgian forces (the so-called "five-day war" or "Russo-Georgian war"). The proximate cause of Russia's incursion was that the Georgian military—which was funded, armed, and trained by the United States—had launched a massive, fourteen-hour artillery and rocket assault on a semi-autonomous Georgian district (South Ossetia). That district borders on Russia and has close ties to it. Of note, the assault occurred just days after the United States led a 2,000-man military exercise inside Georgia. American officials and the U.S. media have sometimes mischaracterized the Russian incursion as an unprovoked invasion.[11]

Aside from the immediate provocation of the Georgian assault, the Russian action was, more generally, a response to the encroachment on Russia's border of Western military power—in particular, that of NATO, spearheaded by the United States. As Colonel Macgregor explained:

> The Russians ultimately intervened in Georgia, and the whole purpose of that intervention was to signal to us [the United States] that they would not tolerate a NATO member on their borders, particularly a member that was hostile to them, as at the time the Georgian Government was. So, I think what we're dealing with now [the war in Ukraine] is exactly the outcome that Ambassador Burns feared when he said no means no.[12]

In late 2013 and early 2014, anti-government protests occurred in Independence Square in Kiev. These protests, which were supported by the United States, were subverted by violent provocateurs. The violence culminated in a coup in which armed, far-right Ukrainian ultra-nationalists took over government buildings and forced the democratically elected pro-Russian president to flee the country. John Mearsheimer, professor of political science at the University of Chicago, described the outcome: "The new government in Kiev was pro-Western and anti-Russian to the core, and it contained four high-ranking members who could legitimately be labeled neofascists."[13]

The United States played a role in these events, though the full extent of its involvement, and whether it directly fomented violence, may never be publicly known. What is known for certain is that since 1991 the United States had poured five billion dollars into its chosen pro-democracy causes in Ukraine,[14] and that it worked behind the scenes, a month before the coup, to determine who would replace the sitting president. This last fact became known when a phone call between Assistant Secretary of State Victoria Nuland and the U.S. ambassador to Ukraine, Geoffrey Pyatt, was hacked or leaked and the audio was posted online. During the call, Nuland used an expletive when referring to the European Union, which created tensions between Washington and European capitals.[15] As Stephen F. Cohen, the late eminent professor of Russian Studies at Princeton and New York University, observed:

> The media predictably focused on the source of the leak and on Nuland's verbal gaffe—"Fuck the EU." But the essential revelation was that high-level U.S. officials were plotting to midwife a new, anti-Russian government by ousting or neutralizing its democratically elected president....[16]

Whatever the exact role of the United States, Russia correctly perceived that America was deeply involved—certainly in laying the foundation for the coup, and possibly in fomenting the violence. In response, and partly out of well-founded concern that the post-coup government or its Western partners might try to block Russia's use of its vital warm-water naval base in Sevastopol, Crimea—access to which Russia had previously negotiated—Russia annexed Crimea. John Mearsheimer writes:

> As former ambassador to Moscow Michael McFaul notes, Mr. Putin's seizure of Crimea was not planned for long: it was an impulsive move in response to the coup that overthrew Ukraine's pro-Russian leader. In fact, until then, NATO expansion was aimed at turning all of Europe into a giant zone of peace, not [at] containing

a dangerous Russia. Once the crisis [of Crimea] started, however, American and European policymakers could not admit they had provoked it by trying to integrate Ukraine into the West. They declared the real source of the problem was Russia's revanchism and its desire to dominate if not conquer Ukraine.[17]

2.

Western Provocations: 2014–2022

Although some or all of the Western provocations just described are widely acknowledged in the West, it is sometimes stated that no new provocations occurred after 2014. This assertion is typically made as part of a broader argument that, since eight years had passed between the 2014 coup and Russia's 2022 invasion, one can disregard claims that Mr. Putin was motivated by national-security concerns. In fact, Western provocations of Russia continued after 2014. Indeed, they arguably intensified, changing in character to become more directly threatening to Russia's security.

After Russia took control of Crimea, the U.S. began a massive program of military aid to Ukraine. According to the U.S. Congressional Research Service, a partial account-ing since 2014, not including most of the military aid initi-ated since the 2022 war began, amounts to over four billion dollars, most coming through the State Department and Department of Defense.[18] One objective of this funding has been "to improve interoperability with NATO"—regardless of the fact that Ukraine is not (yet) in NATO.

In 2016, acting on the prior American abrogation of the anti-ballistic-missile (ABM) treaty, the United States put into operation an ABM site in Romania. Though ostensibly defensive, the ABM system uses the Mark-41 "Aegis" missile launchers, which can accommodate a variety of missile types: not just ABMs, designed to shoot down incoming ballistic missiles, but also—crucially—nuclear-tipped offensive weapons like the Tomahawk cruise missile. Tomahawks have a range of 1,500 miles, can strike Moscow and other targets deep inside Russia, and can carry hydrogen bomb warheads with selectable yields up to 150 kilotons, roughly ten times that of the atomic bomb that destroyed Hiroshima. A similar Aegis site is under construction in Poland and is scheduled for operation in late 2022. The Aegis launchers at each site can accommodate 24 missiles, creating the potential for 48 Tomahawk cruise missiles to be launched at Russia from relatively close range.

Mr. Putin has been adamant that the presence of these offensive-capable Aegis launchers near Russia's border poses a direct danger to Russia. The United States asserts that the ABM sites are intended to stop Europe-targeted warheads coming from Iran or North Korea. But given the launchers' potential to function as offensive threats near Russia's border, an American objective in placing these ABM sites, and conceivably the primary objective, may be to apply additional offensive pressure on Moscow while maintaining plausible denial that any such threat is intended.

The American response to Mr. Putin's concerns about the ABM sites has been to assert that the United States does not intend to configure the launchers for offensive use. But this response requires the Russians to trust America's stated intentions, even in a crisis, rather than to judge the threat by the potential of the systems. It cannot add to Russia's sense of security that the Aegis marketing sheet from Lockheed Martin, which makes the launcher, states, "The system is designed to accept any missile into any cell—a capability that provides unparalleled flexibility."[19]

In 2017, the administration of President Donald J. Trump began to sell lethal weapons to Ukraine. This was a change from the policy of 2014–2017, in which only non-lethal items were sold (for example, body armor and various types of technical gear). The Trump administration described the new sales as "defensive." However, when applied to lethal weapons, the categories "offensive" and "defensive" exist primarily in the mind of the beholder: defensive for those possessing the weapons, offensive for those in the crosshairs. As John Mearsheimer has noted, "these weapons certainly looked offensive to Moscow."[20]

In 2019, the United States unilaterally withdrew from the 1987 treaty on intermediate-range nuclear weapons. I discuss the strategic significance of this step in Chapter 4.

The United States was not alone in starting to sell lethal weapons to Ukraine. Neither was it alone in coordinating militarily with Ukraine, even though Ukraine was not yet a NATO member. Mearsheimer notes:

> Other NATO countries got in on the act, shipping weapons to Ukraine, training its armed forces and allowing it to participate in joint air and naval exercises. In July 2021, Ukraine and America co-hosted a major naval exercise in the Black Sea region involving navies from 32 countries. Operation Sea Breeze almost provoked Russia to fire at a British naval destroyer that deliberately entered what Russia considers its territorial waters.[21]

Even as Western countries, acting outside of NATO, armed, trained, and coordinated with the Ukrainian military,

NATO itself was aggressively pursuing military exercises near Russia. For example, in 2020, NATO conducted a live-fire training exercise inside Estonia. The exercise took place 70 miles from Russia's border, using tactical missiles with ranges up to 185 miles. These weapons can strike Russian territory with minimal warning. In 2021, again in Estonia, NATO fired 24 rockets to simulate an attack on air defense targets inside Russia.[22] Though the West claims such rockets would be used only following an attack by Russia, no prudent military planner would risk a nation's security on the stated intentions of a potential enemy; rather, that planner would look to the offensive capability and location of the hardware.

As it actively pursued these military activities, NATO continued to assert that Ukraine would enter NATO. In a June 2021 meeting in Brussels, NATO reaffirmed its commitment: "We reiterate the decision made at the 2008 Bucharest Summit that Ukraine will become a member of the Alliance."[23] Two months later, in August 2021, the U.S. Secretary of Defense and the Ukrainian Minister of Defense signed the U.S.–Ukraine Strategic Defense Framework.[24] This framework translates the NATO pronouncement into a bilateral (United States–Ukraine) policy decision to change the military facts on the ground starting immediately, regardless whether Ukraine is a NATO member or not. And nine weeks after that signing, the U.S. Secretary of State and the Ukrainian foreign minister signed a similar document, the U.S.–Ukraine Charter on Strategic Partnership.[25] This document, like the one signed by the Defense Department, referenced NATO's declarations of 2008 and 2021, and it operationalized those statements bilaterally, starting immediately, regardless what happened with NATO.

Thus, during the period 2017–2021, we see a confluence of two sets of military activities near Russia's border. First, bilateral military relations, which involved massive shipments of lethal arms, joint Ukrainian–Western training and interoperability exercises inside Ukraine, and the bringing online of offensive-capable missile launchers in Romania, with Poland soon to follow. Second, the military activities of NATO itself, including live-fired missile launches intended to simulate attacks on targets inside Russia. Making matters worse, these simulated attacks emanated from a NATO country on Russia's border that itself was admitted to NATO in disregard of earlier assurances to Moscow. And all this occurred in the context of a reaffirmation that Ukraine would be admitted to NATO. Russia perceived this confluence of military activities as a direct threat to its security. Mearsheimer explained:

> Unsurprisingly, Moscow found this evolving situation intolerable and began mobilizing its army on Ukraine's border to signal its resolve to Washington. But it had no effect, as the Biden administration continued to move closer to Ukraine. This led Russia to precipitate a full-blown diplomatic stand-off in December [2021]. As Sergey Lavrov, Russia's foreign minister, put it: "We reached our boiling point."[26]

Also in December 2021, writing in the journal *Foreign Policy*, the Russian ambassador to the United States noted that NATO was carrying out roughly 40 large training exercises annually near Russia. He warned, "The situation is extremely dangerous." He once again stated what had been made clear 13 years earlier in William Burns' "Nyet means Nyet" cable:

HOW THE WEST BROUGHT WAR TO UKRAINE

> Everything has its limits. If our partners [the U.S. and
> NATO countries] keep constructing military-strategic
> realities imperiling the existence of our country, we will
> be forced to create similar vulnerabilities for them. We
> have come to the point when we have no room to retreat.
> Military exploration of Ukraine by NATO member states
> is an existential threat for Russia.[27]

Mearsheimer described what happened next:

> Russia demanded a written guarantee that Ukraine would
> never become a part of NATO and that the alliance
> remove the military assets it had deployed in eastern
> Europe since 1997. The subsequent negotiations failed, as
> [U.S. Secretary of State] Mr. Blinken made clear: "There
> is no change. There will be no change." A month later,
> Mr. Putin launched an invasion of Ukraine to eliminate
> the threat he saw from NATO.[28]

24

3.
Putting the Shoe on the Other Foot

In considering the 30-year history just described, one must ask: How would U.S. leaders respond if the situation were reversed—say, if Russia or China carried out equivalent steps near U.S. territory? For example, how would Washington respond if Russia established a military alliance with Canada and then set up rocket installations 70 miles from the U.S. border? What would happen if Russia then used those rocket installations to conduct live-fire training exercises to practice destroying military targets inside America? Would U.S. leaders accept verbal assurances from Russia that its intentions were benign?

Of course not. The likely response would be as follows. U.S. military planners and policy makers would look to the offensive potential of the arms and training exercises. They would disregard the stated intentions and would perceive a serious threat. They might interpret the live-fire exercises as signaling an impending Russian attack. The United States would demand that the rockets be removed and, if this demand was not acted on forthwith, the United States might respond with a preemptive attack on the rocket installations, which might in turn precipitate a general war and the possibility of escalation to a thermonuclear exchange. Further, the U.S. leadership, and surely most

U.S. citizens as well, would then ascribe to Russia moral culpability for America's pre-emptive attack, which they would describe as self-defense.

Beginning with the formulation of the Monroe Doctrine almost 200 years ago, the United States has essentially forbidden potentially threatening foreign powers to place military forces in the Western hemisphere. U.S. policy thus reveals a conviction about the strategic importance of geographic proximity in military deployments, irrespective of stated intentions. This understanding is the cornerstone of American foreign policy.

Yet in its relations with Russia, the United States, sometimes alone, sometimes with its NATO allies, acts with blithe disregard of the same principles, even when applied with respect to local geography—that is, right next to Russia. The U.S. withdraws unilaterally from arms control treaties, foments anti-Russian revolutions in countries on Russia's border, and pushes its military forces and training exercises to the edge of Russian territory, justifying these actions on the grounds that Western intentions are benign and that the objective is merely to deter Russian aggression. It does these things without apparent concern for how prudent Russian leaders, military planners, and ordinary Russian citizens might perceive them, or for how such actions might affect Russia's political and military posture and decisions over time. As Colonel Macgregor describes:

> I kept trying to explain to people that for the Russians what happens in Ukraine is an existential matter. Ukraine is not some distant country in North Africa. Ukraine sits right next to Russia. Russia will not tolerate foreign forces and capabilities on the ground inside a country

that is hostile to them that could conceivably threaten their existence. I've drawn the analogy with Mexico, trying to say to people: "Don't you understand what we would do if the Russians or the Chinese or someone else established a force in Mexico?"[29]

In 1962, the Soviets placed nuclear missiles in Cuba, thereby precipitating the Cuban missile crisis. Although not widely known, the Soviet placement of missiles in Cuba was carried out shortly after the United States placed hydrogen bomb–tipped Jupiter missiles in Turkey. Also not well known is that the Soviets ultimately removed their missiles from Cuba, which resolved the crisis, as part of a secret deal between the United States and the Soviet Union, according to which both countries would remove their offending weapons. By agreement, the United States removed its Turkish missiles quietly, months after the Soviets removed theirs from Cuba.

Because the linkage between the missile removals was not made public, many in the West drew a false lesson from the Cuban crisis. They wrongly concluded that America won a high-stakes game of strategic brinkmanship through an unrelenting display of strength and the threat of nuclear escalation. In reality, nuclear war was avoided because of a compromise, one that, in fact, was made possible because President John F. Kennedy had previously fostered a good personal relationship with the Soviet premier and thus could credibly negotiate in good faith and thereby deescalate the situation.[30] Obviously, the situation is very different now.

Finally, an additional word is needed about the question of whether Western nations had promised, in 1990 and 1991, not to expand NATO toward Russia's border.

The issue of Western promises has taken on great importance in the mind of many observers. Some of these observers have argued that, absent formal treaty obligations, no actual promises were made; or they have asserted that promises were made but were not legally binding. Others have asserted that, as a practical matter, NATO has no intention of offering membership to Ukraine during the next few years, making the entire question of Ukraine's membership moot. Here, two points are important.

First, whether or not the eastward expansion of NATO violated formal treaty obligations—it clearly did not—the West's disregard of the assurances it gave Russia bears on the question of whether Mr. Putin and other Russian leaders have felt deceived, humiliated, and disrespected. These Western actions established a baseline distrust, which future Western actions have exacerbated. Second, even if we stipulate, as a mental exercise, that the West had not misrepresented its intentions—that is, if we assume for the sake of discussion that no assurances were ever given—the more important problem, the actual military encroachments of NATO and the West, would be unchanged.

Ultimately, it is not decisive whether assurances were made in 1990–1991. Neither is it decisive whether the military threats emerged via NATO or, outside of NATO, by means of bilateral or multilateral actions between Ukraine and Western countries. Threats are threats—regardless of the words or actions that precede them and regardless of the administrative path by which they come into existence. What is important is the answer to this question: What is the situation on the ground, and how can a nation interested in its survival, and prudent leaders tasked with ensuring that survival, be expected to respond to those threats? That is the point that must be understood when considering the question of Western actions and provocations.

4.
Russian Concerns About a U.S. First Strike

In 2019, the United States, during the administration of President Trump, withdrew from the 1987 Treaty on Intermediate-Range Nuclear Forces, claiming that the Russians had cheated. (Treaty obligations had been accepted by Russia after the dissolution of the Soviet Union, as had been the case with the ABM treaty.) Intermediate-range missiles are defined as surface-to-surface (land-to-land) missiles with a range of between 500 and 5,500 kilometers—longer than battlefield weapons, shorter than long-range weapons like ICBMs. The claim about cheating was technical in nature and, in fact, both the United States and Russia had plausible claims that the other side was violating the spirit, if not the letter, of the treaty.

But whether one, both, or neither country was technically in violation, the key point is that the United States withdrew unilaterally rather than aggressively seeking to resolve the issues. In deciding to do so, the Americans may have sensed a military advantage, because the missiles in question would be placed in Europe, close to Russia, whereas Russia did not have plans to place weapons at equivalent distances from the United States. Further, the allegation of Russian cheating may have been largely a pretext, a way for the United States to quit the treaty so it could deploy intermediate-range missiles directed against China, whose own efforts at nuclear catch-up were not constrained by the 1987 treaty.

China aside, the United States' decision to withdraw may have been driven largely by a narrow focus on achieving a tactical advantage over Russia at the expense of broader strategic dangers. These dangers include: the risk of precipitating a renewed U.S.–Russian nuclear arms race; pushing Russia to adopt a hair-trigger launch policy; stimulating the development of new classes of Russian nuclear weapons; pushing Russia to deploy those new weapons at equivalent distances from U.S. territory; and destabilizing the U.S.–Russian political relationship in ways that could undercut their ability to defuse a nuclear crisis. Major Brennan Deveraux, a U.S. Army strategist specializing in rocket artillery and missile warfare, noted the problem in his January 28, 2022 article at the online military insider website, *War on the Rocks*:

> The Western narrative is straightforward: Theater support [intermediate-range] missiles provide the United States and NATO with new capabilities to better deal with a resurgent Russia and a rising China. But this discourse overlooked the strategic implications of employing these missiles, and neglected any potential Russian response.[31]

Russia had been deeply concerned that new U.S. missiles, placed close to its borders, could increase the chance that, in a crisis, the United States might believe it could carry out a preemptive first strike, decapitating Russian command and control systems and degrading Russia's ability to retaliate. When coordinated with even a partially effective ABM network, intermediate-range weapons thus stimulate Russian concerns that the United States would no longer be deterred. These fears are not merely Russian paranoia. As two members of the German Council on Foreign Relations quoted by Deveraux explained, these missiles "could threaten Moscow's command facilities and limit Russia's military ability to act." Russia thus had much to gain by saving the intermediate-range missile treaty. But the United States stood firm and withdrew.

After the loss of the treaty was a *fait accompli*, Russia sought new, mutual restrictions and moratoria on missile deployments. These potentially could have allowed the United States and Russia to pause their own mutually targeted weapons while allowing them to deploy weapons directed at China. However, the United States dismissed the Russian proposal. Major Deveraux noted that the West's response

> not only failed to address Russia's concerns but treated the reintegration of these missiles [into its force structure] as a foregone conclusion, focusing almost exclusively on the relative advantage that their deployment could provide to the United States and NATO.

Deveraux also described how branches of the U.S. military competed for the new missiles:

> Instead of internal debates on the strategic implications of reintroducing these missiles, the public military discourse centered on which service would have employment and development responsibility. This implied that

the new missiles' eventual employment and forward basing were foregone conclusions.

In fact, during the past year, Mr. Putin repeatedly expressed his concern about such deployments. Deveraux again:

> In October 2021, just as the current Ukraine crisis began, Putin expressed his frustration with the international community regarding his proposed missile moratorium: "Has anyone even reacted to our statement that we will not deploy this kind of missile in the European part if we produce them, if they tell us that no one will do so from the United States or Europe? No. They never responded." He built on these comments in a December press conference, saying "Are we putting our rockets near the borders of the United States? No we're not. It's the U.S. with its rockets coming to our doorstep."

Although it is impossible to know the specific motivations that led Mr. Putin to invade Ukraine, a combination of factors was likely at play: (1) the ongoing arming, training to NATO standards, and integration of the military structures of Ukraine, the United States, and other Western powers through non-NATO arrangements; (2) the ongoing threat that Ukraine would be admitted to NATO; and (3) concern about possible new intermediate-range missile deployments, exacerbated by a concern that the U.S. might deploy Aegis, offensive-capable ABM launchers in Ukraine regardless whether Ukraine was yet a member of NATO.

Regarding this last point, it is possible, given ongoing and progressive military coordination between the United States and Ukraine, that Mr. Putin felt the window to prevent the deployment of offensive-capable Aegis launchers in Ukraine was closing and that, if he were to obviate that threat, he would have to act now. This is all speculative, but it is plausible and consistent with previously stated Russian concerns. But regardless of what specifically led to the invasion, it is clear that the threat of new Aegis deployments added another cup of sand to a sand castle that was already near the point of collapse.

5.
Policy Experts Warned Against NATO Expansion

During the past 30 years, senior U.S. foreign policy experts have repeatedly warned that, in expanding NATO into Eastern Europe, the United States was making a dangerous policy error. In 1997, as NATO was taking a major step toward expansion, George Kennan, perhaps the most eminent American statesman then alive (during the 1940s, he pioneered the policy of "containment" and later served as ambassador to the Soviet Union) warned that "expanding NATO would be the most fateful error of American policy in the entire post-cold-war era." Kennan lamented the senselessness of the entire expansionary project, asking:

> Why, with all the hopeful possibilities engendered by the end of the cold war, should East-West relations become centered on the question of who would be allied with whom and, by implication, against whom in some fanciful, totally unforeseeable and most improbable future military conflict?[32]

A year later, in an interview with Thomas Friedman, the 94-year-old statesman responded to the Senate's ratification of NATO expansion:

> I think it is the beginning of a new cold war. I think the Russians will gradually react quite adversely and it will affect their policies. I think it is a tragic mistake. There was no reason for this whatsoever. No one was threatening anybody else. This expansion would make the Founding Fathers turn over in their graves.[33]

Kennan then added: "Don't people understand? Our differences in the cold war were with the Soviet Communist regime. And now we're turning our backs on the very people who mounted the greatest bloodless revolution in history to remove that Soviet Regime."

Kennan was not alone. Many others — including prominent hawks—also argued against expansion. Among these were Robert McNamara, ex-Secretary of Defense, who planned and implemented massive bombing campaigns during the Vietnam war; Paul Nitze, previously Secretary of the Navy and Secretary of Defense, who had opposed Kennan's policy of static containment, favoring more aggressive attempts to compel the Russians to vacate territories; the crusading anti-Communist Harvard academic Richard Pipes, who had headed a team organized by the CIA to analyze the strategic capabilities and goals of the Soviet Union; ex-CIA chief Robert Gates, who later became Secretary of Defense; Jack F. Matlock, Jr., the second-to-last ambassador to the Soviet Union, who helped negotiate the end of the Cold War; and past ambassadors to Romania, Poland, and West Germany. These and other prominent Washington insiders publicly and vociferously opposed NATO expansion.[34] Yet their counsel was not followed.

In 2015, University of Chicago professor John Mearsheimer began stating publicly that if the West did not stop trying to integrate Ukraine militarily, politically, and economically, the Russians, out of concern for their security, might feel compelled to take military action, including attempting to "wreck" Ukraine as a way to remove it from the equation—a warning that, like Kennan's, was prescient.

Perhaps surprisingly, the basic thrust of the historical argument made by Mearsheimer and other critics of NATO expansion seems to be accepted even by some aggressively Russophobic analysts. A recent interview with Fiona Hill, a Washington insider and outspoken Russia hawk, illustrates this point.[35] In the final paragraph of the interview, published in the online magazine *Politico*, Hill states, "Of course, yes, we've [the United States] also made terrible mistakes." In saying this, Hill seems to be referring to her response to a question posed to her early in the interview. When asked, "So Putin is being driven by emotion right now, not by some kind of logical plan?" Hill corrected the interviewer:

> I think there's been a logical, methodical plan that goes back a very long way, at least to 2007 when he [Putin] put the world, and certainly Europe, on notice that Moscow would not accept the further expansion of NATO. And then within a year in 2008 NATO gave an open door to Georgia and Ukraine. It absolutely goes back to that juncture.

Hill continued,

> Back then I was a national intelligence officer, and the National Intelligence Council was analyzing what Russia was likely to do in response to the NATO Open Door declaration. One of our assessments was that there was a real, genuine risk of some kind of preemptive Russian military action, not just confined to the annexation of

Crimea, but some much larger action taken against Ukraine along with Georgia. And of course, four months after NATO's Bucharest Summit [when the NATO policy about Ukraine and Georgia was announced], there was the invasion of Georgia. There wasn't an invasion of Ukraine then because the Ukrainian government pulled back from seeking NATO membership. But we should have seriously addressed how we were going to deal with this potential outcome and our relations with Russia.

A remarkable aspect of Hill's response is that she asserts several important points that hawkish analysts are typically loath to acknowledge. First, she asserts that in 2007—seven years before Russia's annexation of Crimea—the U.S. intelligence establishment recognized there was a "real, genuine risk" that in response to NATO expansion Russia might annex Crimea. Second, she asserts that in 2007, the intelligence community recognized that NATO expansion might precipitate a broader Russian military action, not just one confined to Crimea, but a "much larger action" taken against both Ukraine and Georgia. Third, Hill asserts that Russia's participation in the Russo-Georgian war was a response to NATO expansion. Finally, Hill states quite directly that, unlike what it did in Georgia, Russia took no action in Ukraine in 2008 because "the Ukrainian government pulled back from seeking NATO membership."

In these points, especially the final one, Hill directly acknowledges the crucial role that NATO expansion and Western military encroachments have played in motivating Russian actions in Ukraine. Thus, it appears that, while arguing for a hawkish position, Hill helps make the case for a perspective much like the one presented by Mearsheimer. However, for reasons hard to fathom, she and like-minded policy gurus give this perspective little or no weight in their decision making. Rather, the perspective seems to fade into the background. Instead of openly acknowledging the untoward consequences of NATO expansion, they attribute Mr. Putin's recent invasion of Ukraine to an unhinged and unprovoked Hitler-like drive for territorial expansion.

Yet even when explicitly portraying Putin as the new Hitler, Hill appears to bring NATO expansion back into the picture. When asked, "So just as the world didn't see Hitler coming, we failed to see Putin coming?" Hill comments:

> We should have. He's been around 22 years now, and he [Putin] has been coming to this point since 2008. I don't think he initially set off to do all this, by the way, but the attitudes towards Ukraine and the feelings that all Ukraine belongs to Russia, the feelings of loss, they've all been there and building up.

It's worth juxtaposing this remark with Hill's previous statement, quoted in full above: "I think there's been a logical, methodical plan that goes back...at least to 2007 when he [Putin] put the world on notice that Moscow would not accept the further expansion of NATO." Considering these two statements together, and focusing on her references to 2007 and 2008, I think it's fair to read Hill as saying that Putin underwent his transformation into the new Hitler *because* of NATO expansion. Whether Putin actually *is* Hitler-like is a different question entirely, but here I am speaking only about the view communicated by Hill.

Further, in assessing Mr. Putin's objectives, Hill notes, "So what Putin wants isn't necessarily to occupy the whole country [of Ukraine], but really to divide it up…. That's something Putin could definitely live with—a fractured, shattered Ukraine with different bits being in different states." This statement should be compared with Mearsheimer's predictions, starting in 2015, that if NATO and the West continued to encroach on Russian territory, Russia might feel the need to, in Mearsheimer's word, "wreck" Ukraine.

Here we see a remarkable parallelism. Both Mearsheimer and Hill appear to believe NATO expansion formed the underlying basis for the transformation of Russian behavior that culminated in the Ukraine war. And both analysts anticipated that, in response to NATO expansion, Russia might seek to "wreck" Ukraine—or, as Hill put it, to turn Ukraine into a "fractured, shattered" nation. I find little fundamental disagreement between Hill and Mearsheimer. But what I do find confusing is that Hill seems not to account in her overall analysis for this important area of agreement between herself and Mearsheimer.

In fact, late in the interview, Hill describes those who point to Western responsibility for the Ukraine crisis as dupes of Russian disinformation: "I mean he [Putin] has got…masses of the U.S. public saying, 'Good on you, Vladimir Putin,' or blaming NATO, or blaming the U.S. for this outcome. This is exactly what a Russian information war and psychological operation is geared towards."

In stating this, Hill seems to disregard her own conclusions about the untoward consequences of NATO expansion. Also, it simply is not accurate that those who hold the United States and NATO responsible for the crisis are saying, in effect, "Good on you, Vladimir Putin." Rather, most of those who emphasize Western culpability for the Ukraine crisis seem to view the Russian invasion of Ukraine as an unmitigated disaster. They see it as an event that—regardless of what the underlying causes might be—has resulted in horrible suffering, destruction, and death. Many critics of NATO, in fact, are also explicitly critical of Putin, even as they emphasize the role of the West in precipitating the crisis.

In forming her view of Russian actions, Hill is, of course, aware of the terrible consequences of the German invasion of Russia during World War II. She even observes in the interview, "Vladimir Putin's own family suffered during the siege of Leningrad." Her comment is accurate, though somewhat of an understatement. As Stephen F. Cohen describes it, "[Putin's] mother and father barely survived near fatal wounds and disease, his older brother died in the long German siege of Leningrad, and several of his uncles perished."[36] Further, the suffering of Mr. Putin's family is representative of that of the Russian nation. Although the precise numbers are unknown, roughly 25 million Soviet citizens died during the German invasions of World War II, with half of those—around 12.5 million—in Russia. That is a death toll equal to about one in every seven Russians then alive.[37]

Yet rather than noting the relevance of this painful history to the question of Russian security; and rather than pointing out how NATO expansion and the encroachment (or, perhaps, in Russian eyes, the *re-encroachment*) of Western military power on Russia's border resonates with that history; and rather than even positing a psychological sensitivity on the part of Mr. Putin based on his own family's experiences—Hill frames Mr. Putin's personal familial experiences as further support for her view that he is motivated by a dangerous and irrational expansionism. Thus, after mentioning Putin's family, she adds sardonically, "yet here [in invading Ukraine] is Vladimir Putin doing exactly the same thing [that Germany did to Russia]." Even when dealing with Mr. Putin's own family traumas, Hill appears to have no room in her analysis for Russian security concerns. There is only Hitler, Nazi Germany, and World War II all over again.

There is no doubt that Russian perceptions of external threats have been deeply influenced by Russia's past. In addition to the German invasions of World War II and World War I, Russia had, a hundred years earlier, been invaded by Napoleon, whose army reached as far as Moscow. Richard Sakwa, professor of Russian and European politics at the University of Kent, England, describes the interplay of this history with the region's geography: "Moscow…doesn't have two major oceans to defend itself. It has no mountains to defend itself. No major rivers. It's set on a vast north Eurasian plain, with no defensible borders, and a constant sense of threat from the West."[38]

Policy hawks such as Hill are, of course, aware of this history and geography. However, instead of viewing them as potential psychological reinforcements for legitimate Russian security concerns, these analysts communicate the view that Mr. Putin is engaged in a Hitlerian land grab, a modern version of a pitiless hunt for *lebensraum,* and that Putin himself is essentially Hitler incarnate—paranoid, living in the imperial past, and driven by an innate Russian militarism. This sort of analysis can be maintained only by disregarding conclusions about NATO expansion that Hill herself has reached and publicly asserted in her interview in *Politico.*

6.

Russophobic Policy Makers
Double Down on Past Mistakes

Notwithstanding the unequivocal failures of the West's policies toward Russia and Ukraine, those responsible for decades of provocative U.S. and NATO actions are now doubling down, asserting that Russia's invasion of Ukraine proves they were correct all along. These analysts assert that the real cause of Russia's invasion is that the United States did not press Russia even harder. The more plausible explanation is that those many U.S. policy experts who predicted that NATO expansion would lead to disaster were correct, and that their predictions are now proving out in terrible ways.

In fact, after the expansion of NATO to Russia's doorstep had begun, George Kennan stated that NATO's decision was a self-fulfilling prophecy. Far from protecting the West, he explained, expansion would lead the U.S. toward war with Russia. And once this outcome occurred, Kennan predicted, proponents of the expansion would say this proved that inherent Russian militarism was the cause. Kennan stated: "Of course there is going to be a bad reaction from Russia, and then [the proponents of expansion] will say that we always told you that is how the

Russians are—but this is just wrong."[39] Kennan's prediction was thus doubly correct: First, about Russian reactions to NATO expansion; second, about the circular, self-justifying response of those Western policy hawks who were on the wrong side of events.

Few in the U.S. media are discussing these things. From watching television and reading the newspapers, one might even imagine that concerns about NATO expansion had never been raised, or that they were of a fringe nature. Although the role of the United States and the NATO countries in creating the crisis in Ukraine should be obvious, many Americans and Europeans have been overcome by a kind of "war fever by proxy," missing the big picture but preoccupied with the quotidian details of battle, driven by a self-righteous anger and a conviction that the best policy is to pour more and more weapons into Ukraine until such time as Mr. Putin cries uncle.

In light of the intensity of this war fever, it should not be surprising that those few U.S. political leaders who have the rare combination of clarity and guts required to openly discuss the background to the Ukraine war have been called traitors. In truth, they are patriots. They are refusing to play the tribal game of "My country can do no wrong." They are recognizing uncomfortable historical facts for what they are and trying to avoid repeating the same mistakes in the future. And they want to discern the implications of those facts for the present, especially in ways that might limit the death and destruction in Ukraine and, simultaneously, reduce the chance of an apocalyptic nuclear confrontation between Russia and the West. Looking at the situation from a recent vantage, John Mearsheimer wrote,

[W]e are in an extremely dangerous situation, and Western policy is exacerbating these risks. For Russia's leaders, what happens in Ukraine has little to do with their imperial ambitions being thwarted; it is about dealing with what they regard as a direct threat to Russia's future. Mr. Putin may have misjudged Russia's military capabilities, the effectiveness of the Ukrainian resistance and the scope and speed of the Western response, but one should never underestimate how ruthless great powers can be when they believe they are in dire straits. America and its allies, however, are doubling down, hoping to inflict a humiliating defeat on Mr. Putin and to maybe even trigger his removal. They are increasing aid to Ukraine while using economic sanctions to inflict massive punishment on Russia, a step that Putin now sees as "akin to a declaration of war."[40]

7.

How Overly Pessimistic Narratives Become Self-Fulfilling Prophecies

The story of an evil, irrational, intrinsically expansionist Russia with a paranoid leader at its helm, opposed by a virtuous United States and Europe, is a confused and strange confabulation, inconsistent with a whole series of directionally aligned events during the past 30 years — events whose significance and meaning should have been readily apparent. In fact, the predominant Western narrative might itself be viewed as a kind of paranoia.

The provocations that the United State and its allies have directed at Russia are policy blunders so serious that, had the situation been reversed, U.S. leaders would long ago have risked nuclear war with Russia. For U.S. leaders to assert otherwise, as they now are doing, represents a dangerous disregard of reality. In some cases, this disregard surely represents willful demagoguery. But for some policy makers it must be well intentioned, occurring for the simple reason that they continue to interpret new facts in light of the same spent narrative.

Major press outlets also bear responsibility. Rather than seeking to contextualize events properly for their readers, the media have trumpeted the government's preferred narrative. Whatever its motivations, the mainstream media have implemented, and continue to implement, a regime of propaganda that misinforms the public and can only be perceived by Russia as an affront to the national character of its people. Online providers of information are doing much the same. In fact, as the Pulitzer Prize–winning journalist and First Amendment lawyer Glenn Greenwald has shown, massive censorship of dissenting views is now occurring at many levels of society in both the United States and Europe.[41]

Although it is difficult to look at the horrific images coming out of Ukraine without revulsion and anger, succumbing to blind emotion and embracing the dominant Western narrative is a dangerous error. It empowers the worst forces in Washington, including the nexus of bureaucratic power and commercial interest that President Eisenhower, a five-star Army general, termed the military-industrial complex, about which he warned the American public in his final televised address as U.S. president. This narrative also enables the most Russophobic and militaristic of European leaders, as well as those with the least guts to stand up to misguided American policies. The narrative clouds the minds of American and European citizens, leading to jingoism and war-mongering.

My primary goal in this book is to correct a false narrative, and for a very practical reason: because false narratives lead to bad outcomes. Narratives are inevitably reflected in behaviors; they are both descriptive and generative. By functioning as models of reality, narratives serve as guides for action. Then, through the dynamic of action and reaction, push and pushback, they can produce the results they allege are already present. In this way, a narrative that is overly pessimistic about the intentions of a potential opponent — what I term a "narrative of suspicion" — can potentiate the very threats it purports to mitigate.

This description underlies the classic dynamic of an arms race that culminates in escalation and war. It instantiates not the paradigm of World War II, with its associated images of implacable expansionism and Western appeasement, but of World War I, in which Germany, Britain, Western Europe, and ultimately America sleep-walked into catastrophe. Yet now, because of the nature of nuclear weaponry, catastrophe can happen more easily, and with more devastating effect.

As with World War I, each side, fearing the worst from the other, seeks to make itself invulnerable through a military strategy that necessarily also has offensive potential—a double-edged strategic sword that policy analysts term a "security dilemma." This is precisely what George Kennan predicted with respect to NATO expansion, and in respect to which he has proven correct. That expansion, which was justified in the name of defense, has been perceived by Russia as an offensive threat and led to actions that are, in turn, perceived by the West as expansionist. In 2014, Richard Sakwa offered a pithy retrospect on the situation that Kennan had anticipated:

> In the end, NATO's existence became justified by the need to manage the security threats provoked by its enlargement. The former Warsaw Pact and Baltic states joined NATO to enhance their security, but the very act of doing so created a security dilemma for Russia that undermined the security of all.[42]

And since Sakwa wrote, the situation has only gotten worse, in good measure because the United States and its allies have carried out a parallel set of military expansions outside of NATO.

Mr. Putin, whatever authoritarian tendencies he might possess, was not born on a set path. In the current zeitgeist, it may be considered heretical to state the obvious: that Mr. Putin, like all human beings, is influenced by a combination of what is within—his psychology, beliefs, and values—and what is without, the dynamic external circumstances that confront him. This is simply a truism. It is likewise a truism that chronic exposure to certain patterns of external events can change a person's inner tendencies, or, at least, selectively magnify some tendencies at the expense of other, sometimes opposite tendencies.

Incrementally, in steps small and large, the West has disregarded Russia's reasonable security concerns, considering them irrelevant, stoking Russian concerns about encirclement and invasion. At the same time, the United States and its European allies have implied that a rational actor would be assuaged by the West's statements of benign intention: that the weapons, training, and interoperability exercises, no matter how provocative, powerful, or close to Russia's borders, are purely defensive and not to be feared. In many instances, Western leaders, especially from the United States, have actively disrespected Mr. Putin, sometimes insulting him to his face.

In doing all this, the West has suggested that Mr. Putin is imagining strategic threats where none in fact exist. This Western framing—which posits a lack of legitimate Russian security concerns coupled with implied and explicit accusations of irrationality—underlies much of the currently dominant narrative. It also underlies the ideological position of the Russia hawks who play such a prominent role in

Washington. In personal relationships, the combination of threatening actions and accusations of paranoia would be considered gaslighting. Is the situation really so different in the realm of international politics?

During times of war and military threat, even the leaders of free countries lean toward authoritarianism. Sensing great danger, they may tighten the reins of power, imposing top-down control and expanding the categories of domestic action and speech that are considered treasonous. It is not extreme to suggest that the provocations described in this book created in the mind of Mr. Putin and other members of the Russian political and military class an evolving sense of siege and emergency. My point is that one must contemplate the possibility that Western actions contributed not only to Russia's foreign policies, but to untoward aspects of Russia's domestic politics as well. In fact, George Kennan predicted this in 1998. NATO expansion, he said, would "have an adverse effect on the development of Russian democracy."[43]

Political actors, both individuals and corporate actors, such as bureaucracies and nations, are not static entities. Rather, the human decisions we call "policies" emerge from a concatenation of conscious intentions; unconscious motivations; accidents of history; and personal, human interactions, including blatantly threatening, humiliating, and disrespectful interactions and words, such as those that have emanated from the mouth of President Biden. And it is quite possible that the actions of the United States and its European allies exerted, and continue to exert, a more profound effect on the policies of Mr. Putin, including his domestic policies, than some are inclined to think.[44]

8.

A Counterfactual History
—and Conclusion

Who bears responsibility for the humanitarian disaster in Ukraine, for the death of thousands of Ukrainians, both civilians and soldiers, and for the impressment of Ukrainian civilians into the military? Who bears responsibility for the destruction of Ukrainian homes and businesses, and for the refugee crisis that is now adding to the one from the Middle East? Who bears responsibility for the deaths of thousands of young men serving in the Russian military, most of whom surely believe, like their Ukrainian counterparts, that they are fighting to protect their nation and their families? Who bears responsibility for the ongoing harm being inflicted on the economies and citizens of Europe and the United States? Who will bear responsibility if disruptions in farming lead to famine in Africa, a continent that depends heavily on the importation of grain from Ukraine and Russia? And finally, who will bear responsibility if the war in Ukraine escalates to a nuclear exchange, and then becomes a full-scale nuclear war?

In a proximal sense, the answer to all these questions is simple: Mr. Putin is responsible. He started the war and, with his military planners, is directing its conduct. He did not have to go to war. Those are facts. But facts must be interpreted with reference to other facts, including those that have long since passed from the headlines, or were never there in the first place. When that is done, it becomes clear that policy makers in the United States and Europe bear significant responsibility for the war.

How one judges the relative responsibilities of Moscow, Washington, and the various European capitals will depend on how one weighs particular historical events, the actions of the individuals involved, and the relative stress one places on proximal and distal causation. Nonetheless, I will venture the judgment that, when all is taken into account, primary responsibility lies with the West, in particular with the United States. I know of no entirely satisfactory way to argue this point; there is no validated methodology for apportioning blame among a range of actors, all of whom have at least some agency, some freedom of choice. But I believe we can gain insight by constructing a counterfactual history, which asks: Where would we be now had the United States acted differently? This is a game of "what if"—and the projections it generates can never be proven or disproven. But this counterfactual sits well with the history of the last 30 years and, to my mind, is both revealing and persuasive.

Had the United States not pushed NATO to the border of Russia; not deployed nuclear-capable missile launch systems in Romania and planned them for Poland and perhaps elsewhere as well; not contributed to the overthrow of the democratically elected Ukrainian government in 2014; not abrogated the ABM treaty and then the intermediate-range nuclear missile treaty, and then disregarded Russian attempts to negotiate a bilateral moratorium on deployments; not conducted live-fire exercises with rockets in Estonia to practice striking targets inside Russia; not coordinated a massive 32-nation military training exercise near Russian territory; not intertwined the U.S. military with that of Ukraine; etc. etc. etc.—had the United States and its NATO allies not done these things, the war in Ukraine probably would not have taken place. I think that is a reasonable assertion.

In fact, I would suggest that had any two or three of the many provocations discussed here not occurred, things would be very different today. I have already used the analogy of a beach castle built with cups of sand. Although one cannot easily predict how much sand, in which configuration, the structure can bear, it is clear that the greater the amount of sand, the higher the piles, and the more precarious the placement, the more unstable the structure will become. I would say that the West piled cups and cups of sand on a structure that a clear-thinking, rational actor would have recognized as likely to eventuate in collapse. The war in Ukraine is one such collapse, and there is no reason to think that more disasters won't follow, regardless how much war planners in the United States imagine they can gut Russia's military capacity.

And even that is not the end of it. The U.S. government, through its words and actions, may have led Ukrainian leaders, and the Ukrainian people, to adopt intransigent positions toward Russia. Instead of pressing and supporting a negotiated peace in the Donbas between Kiev and pro-Russian autonomists, the United States encouraged strongly nationalistic forces in Ukraine. It poured weapons into Ukraine, stepped up military integration and training with the Ukrainian military, refused to renounce plans to incorporate Ukraine into NATO, and may have given the impression to the Ukrainian leaders and people that it might directly go to war with Russia on Ukraine's behalf.

All this may have affected Ukrainian president Volodymyr Zelensky, who won his 2019 election, with over 70 percent popular support, running on a peace platform. Yet in the end he failed to carry through. Even with war looming, he would not compromise for the sake of peace. On February 19, five days before Russia invaded, Mr. Zelensky met in Munich with German Chancellor Olaf Scholz. According to *The Wall Street Journal*, Scholz proposed to broker a peace deal. He told Mr. Zelensky

> that Ukraine should renounce its NATO aspirations and declare neutrality as part of a wider European security deal between the West and Russia. The pact would be signed by Mr. Putin and Mr. Biden, who would jointly guarantee Ukraine's security. Mr. Zelensky said Mr. Putin couldn't be trusted to uphold such an agreement and that most Ukrainians wanted to join NATO. His answer left German officials worried that the chances of peace were fading.[45]

In a recent interview, Richard Sakwa suggested that Mr. Zelensky could have made peace with Russia by speaking just five words: "Ukraine will not join NATO." Sakwa continued: "If Putin was bluffing [about the decisive importance of NATO expansion], call his bluff. Instead…we had this catastrophic war…. It was a frivolous approach to the fate of a nation and, above all, the fate of his own people."[46]

How did an advocate of peace, who had a strong electoral mandate for negotiating an end to the Donbas conflict, come to dig in his heels and gamble on war? I would suggest that absent the foisting of misguided and unrealistic notions on Ukraine by the United States, Ukraine would long ago have worked out a *modus vivendi* with Russia, likely adopting a stance of political neutrality—something that now, and only if it is lucky, Ukraine might yet achieve after the destruction of half its country, the death of thousands, and the displacement and immiseration of millions. There is a venerable history of neutrality in Europe. Both Austria and Finland adopted neutrality toward the Soviet Union and greatly benefited from it. Though the form of government in Moscow has changed, the geo-strategic rationale for neutrality is the same. Why did this not happen with Ukraine?

Shortly after Zelensky was elected in 2019, Stephen F. Cohen suggested in an interview that Zelensky would need the active support of the United States to overcome pressure—including threats against his life—from Ukraine's far right. Without this support, Cohen predicted, Mr. Zelensky would not be able to seek peace:

> [T]he new president of Ukraine, Zelensky, ran as a peace candidate.... He won an enormous mandate to make peace. So, that means he has to negotiate with Vladimir Putin.... But his willingness—and this is what's important and not well reported here [in the United States]—his willingness to deal directly with Putin... actually required considerable boldness on [the part of] Zelensky because there are opponents of this in Ukraine and they are armed. Some people say they are fascist, but they are certainly ultra-nationalist, and they have said that they will remove and kill Zelensky if he continues along this line of negotiating with Putin.... Zelensky cannot go forward...unless America has his back. Maybe that won't

be enough, but unless the White House encourages this diplomacy, Zelensky has no chance....[47]

To my knowledge, Zelensky never received any substantial American support to pursue his peace agenda. Instead, he was subjected to repeated visits by leading American politicians and State Department officials, all of whom spouted a theoretical principle of absolute Ukrainian freedom, defined as the "right" to join NATO and to establish a U.S. military outpost on Russia's border. In the end, this "freedom" was worse than a pipe dream. Although it advanced the aims of the United States—or, more accurately, the interests of certain American political, military, and financial factions—it destroyed Ukraine.

Even from a blinkered American perspective, the whole Western plan was a dangerous game of bluff, enacted for reasons that are hard to fathom. Ukraine is not, by any stretch of the imagination, a vital security interest of the United States. In fact, Ukraine hardly matters at all. From an American perspective — and I say this with no disrespect for the Ukrainian people — Ukraine is irrelevant. Ukraine is no more important to the citizens of the United States than any one of fifty other countries that most Americans, for perfectly understandable reasons, couldn't find on a map without a lot of random searching. So yes, Ukraine is irrelevant to America. And if the leaders of the United States and NATO had acknowledged that obvious fact, none of this would be happening.

In contrast, for Russia—with its 1,200-mile shared border and its history of three major land-route invasions from the West, the most recent of which, during World War II, caused the death of *roughly 13 percent of the entire*

Russian population — Ukraine is the most vital of vital interests.

The existential threat that Russia perceives from a Western-armed, trained, and militarily integrated Ukraine should have been clear to Washington from the start. Really, what sane person could believe that putting a Western arsenal on Russia's border would not produce a powerful response? What sane person could believe that placing this arsenal would enhance American security? And if any uncertainty remained, it should have been removed in 2008 when the U.S. Ambassador to Russia, William Burns, who now heads Mr. Biden's CIA, cabled to Washington that, for Russia, Ukraine was the reddest of red lines. It does not take a rocket scientist to understand why. Yet this transparent reality seems opaque to many in the U.S. Departments of State and Defense, in NATO and the media, and to the sitting American president.

So, where does this leave the citizens of the United States and its European allies?

Frankly, it leaves them—*us*—in a very bad spot. It is a spot that not only is exceedingly dangerous, putting the entire world at risk of nuclear war: it is one that could only have been arrived at through a level of American governmental stupidity and blindness, and, among the leaders of Europe, a level of deference and cowardice, that is almost inconceivable. In a recent interview, Gilbert Doctorow was asked what he thinks American citizens most need to know about the war. His reply: "Your lives are in danger." He continued,

> Mr. Putin has been on record that he does not contem-
> plate a world without Russia. And if the American intent

is to destroy Russia, then the American intent will be self-destruction.... [America] is facing an existential threat of its own making. And the escape from this threat is in front of everybody's nose: it's to do a deal with Mr. Putin....[48]

Policy makers in Washington and the European capitals—along with the captured, craven media that uncritically amplify their nonsense—are now standing up to their hips in a barrel of viscous mud. How those who were foolish enough to step into that barrel will find the wisdom to extricate themselves before they tip the barrel and take the rest of us down with them is hard to imagine.

Citations

All links checked and functioning as of July 2, 2022.

1 Chas Freeman, interview, 24 March 2022 <https://thegrayzone.com/2022/03/24/us-fighting-russia-to-the-last-ukrainian-veteran-us-diplomat/>.

2 On Mr. Putin's February 27 statement, see <https://www.armscontrol.org/act/2022-03/news/putin-orders-russian-nuclear-weapons-higher-alert>. On current and historical Defcon levels, with explanation for reasons, see <https://www.defconlevel.com/> and <https://www.defconlevel.com/history.php>.

3 Avril Haines, testimony, 10 May 2022 <https://www.c-span.org/video/?c5014371/us-believes-russian-president-putin-preparing-prolonged-conflict#>.

4 Gilbert Doctorow, interview <https://www.youtube.com/watch?v=CHbHx44ohTE>, starting at 56:30.

5 "NATO Expansion: What Gorbachev Heard." National Security Archive, George Washington University <https://nsarchive.gwu.edu/briefing-book/russia-programs/2017-12-12/nato-expansion-what-gorbachev-heard-western-leaders-early>.

6 "Deal or No Deal? The End of the Cold War and the U.S. Offer to Limit NATO Expansion." *International Security*, Vol. 40, No. 4 (Spring 2016), pp. 7–44 <https://www.belfercenter.org/sites/default/files/files/publication/003-ISEC_a_00236-Shifrinson.pdf>.

7   "Author Chat: Joshua Itzkowitz Shifrinson," 5 August
    2016, Harvard Kennedy School Belfer Center for Science
    and International Affairs <https://www.belfercenter.org/
    publication/author-chat-joshua-itzkowitz-shifrinson>.

8   See, for example: <https://direct.mit.edu/isec/article-
    abstract/42/1/186/12171/NATO-Enlargement-Was-There-
    a-Promise?> and <https://jackmatlock.com/2014/04/nato-
    expansion-was-there-a-promise/>.

9   Interview, Douglas Macgregor, 31 March 2022 <https://
    scotthorton.org/interviews/3-31-22-colonel-douglas-
    macgregor-the-us-is-deliberately-ignoring-the-path-to-
    peace-in-ukraine/>, 18:05.

10 "Nyet Means Nyet: Russia's NATO Enlargement Redline," 1
    February 2008, confidential cable posted at wikileaks <https://
    wikileaks.org/plusd/cables/08MOSCOW265_a.html>.

11 According to an independent investigation commissioned
    by the European Union (EU) ("Independent International
    Fact-Finding Mission on the Conflict in Georgia, Volume
    I" <https://www.mpil.de/files/pdf4/IIFFMCG_Volume_
    I2.pdf>), "Open hostilities began with...a massive Georgian
    artillery attack" [p.19] involving "indiscriminate attacks by
    Georgian forces" on populated, non-military areas using
    both "multiple launch rocket systems and artillery pieces"
    [p. 28]. The EU report declared the Georgian attack illegal
    [p. 22] and implied that the entry of Russian troops into
    Georgia may have been legal under international law as a
    response to the death of Russian peacekeepers [p. 23] who
    were stationed in South Ossetia by international agreement.
    At the same time, the EU investigation stated, "all sides to
    the conflict—Georgian forces, Russian forces and South
    Ossetian forces—committed violations of International
    Humanitarian Law and Human Rights Law" [p. 26] and
    indicated that, while the Georgian assault was a watershed
    moment, it was part of a broader, complex context, with
    many phases and elements, for which it was not possible to

assign overall responsibility to any one party [pp. 31-32].
For additional background, see Gordon M. Hahn, *Ukraine
Over the Edge*, McFarland & Company: Jefferson, North
Carolina, 2018, especially pp. 106–111; and Richard
Sakwa, *Frontline Ukraine*, I.B. Tauris: London, 2015,
index entries for "Russo-Georgian war" and "Saakashvili,
Mikheil."

12 Interview, Douglas Macgregor, 31 March 2022, at 17:35, link
above.

13 "Why the Ukraine Crisis is the West's Fault," *Foreign Affairs*,
September/October 2014 <https://www.mearsheimer.
com/wp-content/uploads/2019/06/Why-the-Ukraine-
Crisis-Is.pdf> p. 4. For additional details on the role of
the far-right, including neo-Nazis, see the peer reviewed
work of Ivan Katchanovski, for example: "The far right, the
Euromaidan, and the Maidan massacre in Ukraine," *Labor
and Society*, 2019, pp. 1–25 <https://in-this-together.com/
UKC/RS-Maidan.pdf?x38956 > and < https://uottawa.
academia.edu/IvanKatchanovski > or his writing for a
popular audience, for example "The hidden origin of the
escalating Ukraine-Russia conflict: Events of the Maidan
massacre shaped one of the most controversial hours in
European history since the end of the Cold War," 22 January
2022 <https://canadiandimension.com/articles/view/the-
hidden-origin-of-the-escalating-ukraine-russia-conflict >.
See also Gordon M. Hahn, *Ukraine Over the Edge*, as above,
especially chapters 6 and 7.

14 "U.S.-Ukraine Foundation Presents, Ukraine in Washington
2013, Address by Assistant Secretary of State Victoria
Nuland, 13 December 2013" <https://www.youtube.com/
watch?v=U2fYcHLouXY>, at 7:45.

15 "'Fuck the EU': US diplomat Victoria Nuland's phonecall
leaked—video," *The Guardian*, 7 February 2014 <https://
www.theguardian.com/world/video/2014/feb/07/eu-us-
diplomat-victoria-nuland-phonecall-leaked-video> and

"Ukraine crisis: Transcript of leaked Nuland-Pyatt call," BBC News, 7 February 2014 <https://www.bbc.com/news/world-europe-26079957>. Also bearing on the question of the Maidan protests, a 2013 USAID public opinion survey in Ukraine found that the desire to affiliate with the EU was far from unanimous: "Thirty-seven percent would like Ukraine to take steps to join the European Union, 33% prefer the Customs Union and 15% say Ukraine should join neither of these blocs. On another question, 34% say that Ukraine should have closer economic relations with Russia, 35% say it should have closer economic relations with Europe and 17% say it should have good relations with both." Quoted from the USAID's "IFES Public Opinion in Ukraine 2013 Key Findings," p. 3 <https://www.ifes.org/sites/default/files/ifes_public_opinion_in_ukraine_2013_key_findings_public.pdf>. These survey results suggest that to the extent the Maidan protests were a response to the ultimate rejection of the association agreement with the EU, they represented a mobilized plurality, not a majority of the Ukrainian population. The majority of the population wished to maintain close trade relations with Russia, but this was excluded by the terms of the EU association agreements. On this last point, see Stephen F. Cohen, *War With Russia?* Hot Books: New York. 2019/2022, p. 17.

16 Stephen F. Cohen, *War With Russia?*, as above, p. 22. In this quotation, I have taken the liberty of smoothing the text by removing Cohen's scare quotes from "leak," "gaff," and "midwife." For two brief, highly readable chapters in *War With Russia?* that discuss the protests and coup and place them into the broader context of American foreign policy toward Russia, see pp. 136–146. A fine reading of this book is available on Audible.

17 "John Mearsheimer on why the West is principally responsible for the Ukrainian crisis," Invited Commentary, 11 March 2022, *The Economist*, <https://www.economist.

com/by-invitation/2022/03/11/john-mearsheimer-on-why-the-west-is-principally-responsible-for-the-ukrainian-crisis>. For an excellent, comprehensive video lecture by Dr. Mearsheimer, see "The causes and consequences of the Ukraine war," given at the European University Institute, Florence, Italy, June 16, 2022 <https://www.youtube.com/watch?v=qciVozNtCDM&t=125s>.The talk itself begins at 10:20 and runs for an hour. The full text of the lecture can be found at <https://nationalinterest.org/feature/causes-and-consequences-ukraine-crisis-203182>.

18 Congressional Research Service, "In Focus" series, 28 March 2022, "U.S. Security Assistance to Ukraine." The 29 April 2022 update of this document provides insight into some of the weapons being supplied to Ukraine <https://crsreports.congress.gov/product/pdf/IF/IF12040?loclr=blogloc>.

19 "MK 41 Vertical Launch System," product card, Lockheed Martin <https://www.lockheedmartin.com/content/dam/lockheed-martin/rms/documents/naval-launchers-and-munitions/MK41-VLS-product-card.pdf>.

20 11 March 2022, *The Economist*, as above.

21 11 March 2022, *The Economist*, as above.

22 "Rocket Artillery Can Keep Russia Out of the Baltics," Brennan Deveraux, 20 May 2021, *War on the Rocks* [website] <https://warontherocks.com/2021/05/rocket-artillery-can-keep-russia-out-of-the-baltics/>.

23 "Brussels Summit Communiqué, Issued by the Heads of State and Government participating in the meeting of the North Atlantic Council in Brussels 14 June 2021" <https://www.nato.int/cps/en/natohq/news_185000.htm>, paragraph 69.

24 "Fact-Sheet—U.S.–Ukraine Strategic Defense Framework August 31, 2021" <https://media.defense.gov/2021/Aug/31/2002844632/-1/-1/0/US-UKRAINE-STRATEGIC-DEFENSE-FRAMEWORK.PDF>.

25 "U.S.-Ukraine Charter on Strategic Partnership," Media Note, Office of the Spokesperson, 10 November 2021 <https://www.state.gov/u-s-ukraine-charter-on-strategic-partnership/>.

26 11 March 2022, *The Economist*, as above.

27 "An Existential Threat to Europe's Security Architecture?", Anatoly Antonov, 30 December 2021 < https://foreignpolicy.com/2021/12/30/russia-ukraine-nato-threat-security/>.

28 11 March 2022, *The Economist*, as above.

29 Douglas Macgregor, Interview, 31 March 2022, as above, 26:28.

30 Among many other sources, "U.S. Nuclear Weapons in Turkey, pt. 2," *Jstor Daily*, Matthew Wills, 28 October 2019 <https://daily.jstor.org/us-nuclear-weapons-turkey-part-2/>.

31 "Why Intermediate-Range Missiles Are a Focal Point in the Ukraine Crisis," Brennan Deveraux, *War on the Rocks* [website], 28 January 2022 <https://warontherocks.com/2022/01/why-intermediate-range-missiles-are-a-focal-point-in-the-ukraine-crisis/>.

32 "A Fateful Error," George F. Kennan, 5 February 1997, *The New York Times* <https://www.nytimes.com/1997/02/05/opinion/a-fateful-error.html>.

33 "Foreign Affairs; Now a Word From X," Thomas L. Friedman, 2 May 1998, *The New York Times* <https://www.nytimes.com/1998/05/02/opinion/foreign-affairs-now-a-word-from-x.html>.

34 See for example, the following: "I was there: NATO and the origins of the Ukraine crisis," Jack F. Matlock Jr., *Responsible Statecraft* [website], 15 February 2022 <https://responsiblestatecraft.org/2022/02/15/the-origins-of-the-ukraine-crisis-and-how-conflict-can-be-avoided/>; "Should NATO Grow? A Dissent," Richard T. Davies, 21

September 1995, *The New York Review of Books* <https://
www.nybooks.com/articles/1995/09/21/should-nato-
growa-dissent/>; and the detailed twitter thread at <https://
archive.ph/Fllhu>.

35 "'Yes, He Would': Fiona Hill on Putin and Nukes," 28
February 2022, *Politico* <https://www.politico.com/
news/magazine/2022/02/28/world-war-iii-already-
there-00012340>.

36 Stephen F. Cohen, *War With Russia?*, p. 7, as above.

37 Wikipedia entry on "World War II casualties of the Soviet
Union" <https://en.wikipedia.org/wiki/World_War_II_
casualties_of_the_Soviet_Union#Estimate>.

38 Richard Sakwa, Interview, 5 December 2021 <https://
soundcloud.com/pushbackshow/war-in-ukraine-nato-
expansion-drives-conflict-with-russia>.

39 *The New York Times*, Thomas Friedman interview, 2 May
1998, as above.

40 11 March 2022, *The Economist*, as above.

41 "Western Dissent from US/NATO Policy on Ukraine is
Small, Yet the Censorship Campaign is Extreme, " Glenn
Greenwald, 13 April 2022 <https://greenwald.substack.
com/p/western-dissent-from-usnato-policy?s=r>.

42 Richard Sakwa, *Frontline Ukraine*, as above, p. 4.

43 *The New York Times*, Thomas Friedman interview, 2 May
1998, as above.

44 For an interesting speculative discussion of the role of soft
factors in international relations as it might pertain to Mr.
Putin, see "Inside Putin's Head," Nonzero Newsletter, 8
March 2022 <https://nonzero.substack.com/p/inside-putins-
head?s=r> and this associated podcast interview, "Russia,
Putin, and the Psychology of Status (Robert Wright &
Steven Ward)," *The Wright Show*, 24 February 2022 <https://

podcasts.apple.com/us/podcast/russia-putin-and-the-psychology-of-status/id505824847?i=1000552544712>.

45 "Vladimir Putin's 20-Year March to War in Ukraine—and How the West Mishandled It," *The Wall Street Journal*, updated 1 April 2022 <https://www.wsj.com/articles/vladimir-putins-20-year-march-to-war-in-ukraineand-how-the-west-mishandled-it-11648826461>.

46 Richard Sakwa, interview, 21 April 2022 <https://www.youtube.com/watch?v=4PBVa4XJEFE>. The relevant segment begins at 16:35 and continues to the end of the interview.

47 Stephen F. Cohen, interview, 13 November 2019 <https://thegrayzone.com/2019/11/13/ukrainegate-impeachment-saga-worsens-us-russia-cold-war/>, at 02:00.

48 Gilbert Doctorow, interview, 28 February 2022 <https://www.youtube.com/watch?v=1c0yYxVIuy0> at 39:40.

Index

About the Author

Benjamin Abelow is a researcher and writer who holds a B.A. in European History from the University of Pennsylvania and an M.D. from the Yale University School of Medicine. He previously worked in Washington, D.C., lecturing, writing, and lobbying Congress about nuclear arms policy. His other areas of interest include the academic study of religion and the psychology of trauma. Emails can be sent to b.abelow.2022@gmail.com. To help ensure that the email passes through the spam filter, please write "Ukraine Book" in the subject line.

Note to the Reader

If you found this book of value, please consider reviewing it at Amazon, Barnes & Noble, Goodreads, Indigo, and other book-related platforms. To help others find the book, consider sharing information about it on social media and with your email networks. If you'd like to purchase this book in quantity for distribution to your organization, or if you'd like to sponsor the book's translation into a language other than English, please contact the publisher at info@SilandPress.com.

Reader's Notes

Made in United States
Orlando, FL
07 October 2022